WHERE DO GOODS COME FROM?

How Is Gasoline Made and Sold?

Derek Miller

Cavendish Square
New York

Published in 2020 by Cavendish Square Publishing, LLC
243 5th Avenue, Suite 136, New York, NY 10016

First Edition

Website: cavendishsq.com

Library of Congress Cataloging-in-Publication Data

Names: Miller, Derek L., author.
Title: How is gasoline made and sold? / Derek Miller.
Description: First edition. | New York, NY : Cavendish Square Publishing, LLC, 2020. | Series: Where do goods come from? | Includes bibliographical references and index. | Audience: Grades 2 to 5.
Identifiers: LCCN 2019013225 (print) | LCCN 2019013977 (ebook) | ISBN 9781502650351 (ebook) | ISBN 9781502650344 (library bound) | ISBN 9781502650320 (pbk.) | ISBN 9781502650337 (6 pack)
Subjects: LCSH: Gasoline--Juvenile literature. | Gasoline industry--Juvenile literature. | Petroleum--Refining.
Classification: LCC TP692.2 (ebook) | LCC TP692.2 .M55 2020 (print) | DDC 665.5/3827--dc23
LC record available at https://lccn.loc.gov/2019013225

Editor: Caitlyn Miller
Copy Editor: Denise Larrabee
Associate Art Director: Alan Sliwinski
Designer: Christina Shults
Production Coordinator: Karol Szymczuk
Photo Research: J8 Media

The photographs in this book are used by permission and through the courtesy of: Cover Pan Demin/Shutterstock.com; p. 5 My Lit'l Eye/Shutterstock.com; p. 8 Smallcreative/Shutterstock.com; p. 9 Kanok Sulaiman/Shutterstock.com; p. 11 Tomas Sereda/iStockphoto.com; p. 12 Andrew Ostry/Shutterstock.com; p. 15 Robert Pernell/Shutterstock.com; p. 16 Eddie Seal/Bloomberg/Getty Images; p. 19 Nightman/Shutterstock.com; p. 20 Keith Wood/Getty Images; p. 23 Pieter Beyl/Wikimedia Commons/File:Evolution of crude oil price.png/CC BY-SA 3.0; p. 25 Dekadi/iStockphoto.com; p. 26 Car Culture/Getty Images; p. 27 Extreme Photographer/Getty Images.

Printed in the United States of America

Table of Contents

Chapter 1

Sourcing Gasoline

Every day, people have to get to work and school. Lots of people take cars and buses. Cars and buses need fuel. Gasoline is what makes them go. Without gasoline, it would be hard for people to get from place to place.

Crude Oil

Making gasoline is a long and difficult process. There are many steps. Often, these steps take place in different parts of the world.

The first step is getting crude oil. Crude oil is the raw material that gasoline comes from. Crude oil is a **fossil fuel**. Other fossil fuels are coal and natural gas. All fossil fuels are made by the same natural process.

Big drills and pumps get crude oil out of the ground.

Hundreds of millions of years ago, plants and animals died. Their remains were buried in Earth's crust, the outer layer of the planet. Heat from deep in Earth and the weight of the ground above turned these remains into fossil fuels.

Coal and natural gas are often burned to create electricity that powers homes and businesses. Crude oil is not very easy to use. It is **refined** to make many kinds of fuel, including gasoline.

Fossil Fuels and the Environment

Humans need fossil fuels to power technology. Most electricity comes from coal and natural gas. Gasoline and other fuels made from crude oil power most vehicles like cars and buses. Without fossil fuels, life as we know it would not be possible.

DID YOU KNOW?

Crude oil bubbles out of the ground in some places. People have used this sticky substance to make roads and buildings.

Yet fossil fuels are not all good. Burning fossil fuels to create energy creates pollution. Pollution harms the environment. It can make the air and water unhealthy. Pollution can even kill plants and animals.

Burning fossil fuels, including products made from them, like gasoline, releases **carbon dioxide**. Carbon dioxide is a gas. It is all around us in the air. Carbon dioxide is not harmful to breathe in, but it is a **greenhouse gas**. Greenhouse gases trap heat on Earth. Since humans started burning fossil fuels, carbon dioxide levels have gone up. As a result, Earth is getting hotter and hotter. Scientists call this global warming. It causes us to have more extreme weather like floods.

Because of global warming, people are looking for new sources of energy. In the future, clean

Solar panels are a source of clean energy.

energy like solar and wind energy might replace fossil fuels. Clean energy does not produce greenhouse gases.

Crude Oil Around the World

Crude oil lies underground. Some countries have very little crude oil. Other countries have a lot. Countries with large reserves of crude oil make a lot of money selling it. Businesses **extract** crude oil from the ground. Drills pierce the ground, and pipes are used to pump oil to the surface.

Many of the world's crude oil reserves are in the Middle East. This region of the world is rich in crude oil. Countries like Saudi Arabia, Iran, and Iraq export, or sell, crude oil to other countries. Some countries outside the Middle East also have a lot of crude oil. Canada, the United States, and Russia have large reserves.

Drilling for oil happens on oil rigs all around the world.

DID YOU KNOW?

Crude oil is measured in barrels. One barrel is equal to 42 gallons (159 liters)!

Chapter 2

Making Gasoline

Once crude oil is extracted from the ground, it needs to be refined. The crude oil is shipped to refineries around the world. Refineries are huge groups of buildings. They turn crude oil into gasoline and other fuels.

Refining Crude Oil

Crude oil is made up of different components. Components are parts of a whole. The first step in refining crude oil is separating the components. The crude oil is slowly heated. As it heats up, the

Oil refineries make gasoline out of crude oil.

components are separated. Gasoline is made from one component. Other components make different things like diesel and asphalt. Diesel is another fuel used in vehicles like trucks. Asphalt is a black, sticky substance used to make roads.

Oil refining causes air pollution. Toxic, or very harmful, **by-products** are created during the refining process and get into the air.

Asphalt is made from crude oil.

By-products aren't the only danger to the environment. Sometimes, oil spills occur. Oil spills can happen during extraction if an oil well has problems. Spills can also occur when oil is being carried to a refinery. Oil spills harm the environment. They often happen at sea. The crude oil harms the living things it touches. When oil spills happen near people, it can poison drinking water, making it unsafe to drink.

Gasoline Additives

After the crude oil is separated into gasoline and other components, there are still more steps to complete. The gasoline made for cars has many **additives**. Additives are put into the gasoline to make it work better.

Some additives reduce pollution. Ethanol is added to American gasoline. It makes gasoline release slightly lower amounts of greenhouse gases.

Other additives protect a car's engine. Gasoline powers a car by burning in the engine. When gasoline burns too soon, it can damage the engine over time. Some additives prevent gasoline from burning too soon. They increase the octane rating of the gasoline. The higher the octane rating, the less likely the gasoline will burn early.

DID YOU KNOW?

Crude oil is also called petroleum. Things made from crude oil are called petroleum products.

In the United States, gasoline additives change depending on the season. Gas stations sell winter blend gasoline in cold months. They sell summer blend gasoline in hot months. Summer blend gasoline burns cleaner because of its additives. Winter blend gasoline lets a car start easier in cold weather.

Diesel and Other Fuels

Some vehicles run on diesel, not gasoline. Diesel powers most tractor trailers and buses in the United States. Like gasoline, diesel is refined from

DID YOU KNOW?

Millions of Americans work in the oil and natural gas industry. In states like Texas and Oklahoma, more than one in ten workers are part of this industry.

Most big trucks run on diesel, not gasoline.

crude oil. However, diesel is easier to produce than gasoline. This often makes diesel cheaper to make than gasoline. However, diesel is sometimes more expensive to buy in countries such as the United States.

Airplanes run on aviation fuel. Aviation fuel is very close to diesel. It has slightly different additives. One kind of aviation fuel is jet fuel. Jet fuel has additives that make it perfect for powering fast-moving jets. However, jets go so fast because of their engines, not their fuel.

Here, workers drill for oil in Texas.

Large ships run on fuel oil. Fuel oil is mostly made up of by-products from refining crude oil. Fuel oil is inexpensive because it is made of by-products. It is very dirty. Burning it pollutes the environment.

Oil and Jobs

Extracting and refining crude oil takes a lot of work. Many people make a living doing it. Some people work on an oil rig, which is the place where oil drilling happens. They make sure the crude oil is extracted from the ground safely.

Other people work at oil refineries. They are in charge of the complicated process of refining crude oil.

Many other people owe their jobs to the oil industry. Truck drivers and the crews of ships move crude oil and gasoline around the world. If it weren't for the oil industry, they wouldn't have jobs.

Chapter 3

Selling Gasoline

Most **goods** are marketed. Sellers try to convince people to buy goods using commercials and other advertisements. Gasoline isn't marketed as much. That's because people with cars need gasoline. Unless they own an electric car, they have to buy gasoline somewhere.

Getting to the Pump

Gasoline is sold at gas stations around the world. It takes a lot of work for the gas to end up there. After petroleum is extracted from the ground, it goes to a refinery. If it needs to cross an ocean, huge oil tankers carry it. Otherwise, trains, trucks, or pipelines move the petroleum.

Oil tankers carry petroleum across oceans.

Pipelines don't need fuel like a truck or ship does. However, if pipelines leak, the petroleum that comes out can harm the environment nearby.

Most refineries in the United States are on the coasts. This makes it easy for tankers to unload petroleum near the refinery. Texas and Louisiana

DID YOU KNOW?

The United States is one of the top countries in the world when it comes to car ownership. About 88 percent of Americans own a car.

This big oil refinery is in Port Arthur, Texas.

have some of the biggest refineries. Once the petroleum is refined, the gasoline is sent to gas stations. Most gasoline is delivered by truck. Sometimes, trains and pipelines are used to carry it part of the way.

Gas stations try to get business by competing to offer the lowest price. Low prices bring in more customers. However, gas stations can only change the price a little. Many issues are outside of their control. For example, gas is taxed. Every time a person buys a gallon of gasoline in the United States, about fifty cents goes to the government. Most of this money is used for roads. Roads need to be fixed all the time.

Supply and Demand

The biggest factor that shapes the price of gasoline is supply and demand. Supply and demand affect the price of most things. Demand is how much of something people want to buy. When people really want or need something, demand is high. When people don't want it, demand is low. Supply is how much of something is for sale in the world. Rare things, like famous works of art, are in low supply. Common things, like paper, are in high supply.

Supply and demand both change a good's price. Low demand and high supply make a good cost less. There is plenty to go around, and few people want it. High demand and low supply make a good cost more. People will spend more money when they really want something and there is not enough to go around.

The price of gasoline changes a lot due to the supply and demand of crude oil. Some years, there is a lot of crude oil available. The price of gasoline drops since supply is high. Other years, there is a low supply. A problem like a war might

DID YOU KNOW?

Not everyone calls gasoline "gas." Outside of the United States and Canada, gasoline is usually called "petrol."

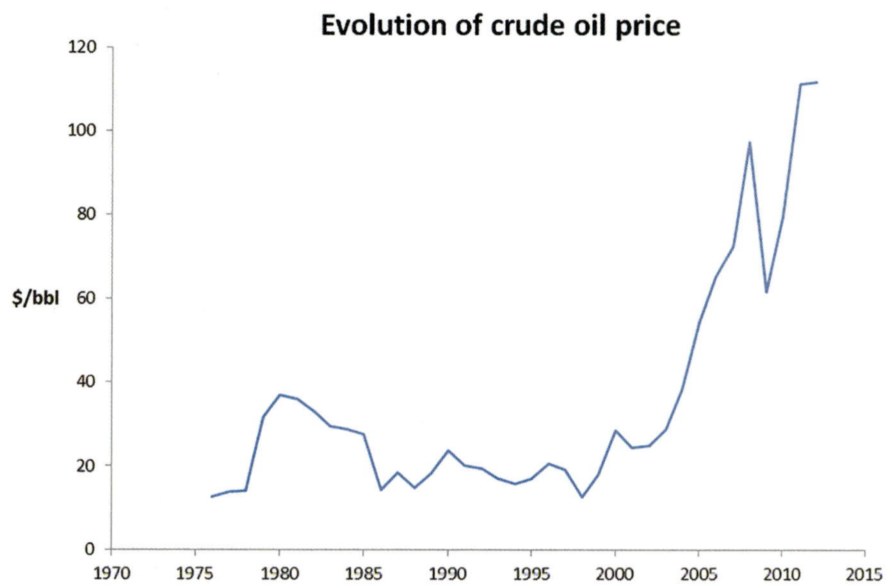

This graph shows that the price of crude oil (in dollars per barrel) has gone up a lot over time.

stop crude oil extraction in some places. Then, the price of gasoline goes up. Supply and demand are responsible for the price of gasoline at the pump.

Chapter 4

Global Connections

Gasoline and other fuels link countries around the world. They power the trucks, ships, and airplanes that carry goods and people. Without gasoline and other fuels, people couldn't travel so quickly and easily.

A World Market

Refining crude oil also connects people around the world. Crude oil is often extracted in one country and shipped to another. There, the crude oil is refined. Sometimes, it is then shipped to yet another country.

People in all these different places have jobs that help with the process. Many oil companies have workers around the world. They get to know people from other countries in their work. Making gasoline brings people together.

It takes a lot of fuel to power this container ship! Container ships move goods around the world.

Moving Forward

The oil industry is changing. Companies now try to limit the pollution that comes from extracting and refining petroleum. However, they cannot get rid of all the pollution.

For this reason, car companies try to help too. They make their cars fuel efficient. "Fuel efficient" means that cars can run just as far on less gasoline. This reduces pollution. It also makes it so

This car is from the 1970s. Older cars aren't as fuel efficient as cars today.

a car's owner pays less for gasoline because they need less of it.

A car's fuel efficiency is measured in miles per gallon: how many miles a car can go on one gallon of gasoline. In 2018, cars averaged 25 miles per gallon (11 kilometers per liter). For each gallon (or liter) of gasoline, a car can drive about 25 miles (11 km). In 1975, cars averaged just 14 miles per gallon (6 kpl). Cars needed a lot more gas to go the same

DID YOU KNOW?

Some countries have frequent power blackouts. Households and businesses own gasoline generators to make their own power.

distance. Better fuel efficiency helps the environment—and saves drivers money.

Electric cars need to be charged. They don't need gasoline.

Companies and scientists everywhere are looking for alternative fuels. As people extract more and more fossil fuels, the supply shrinks. Companies turn to other methods like **fracking**. Fracking extracts crude oil and natural gas that is hard to reach. However, it can cause earthquakes and pollution.

One day, we may run out of fossil fuels. Also, global warming will get worse over time if we keep using these fuels as much as we are now. For these reasons, alternative fuels are being tested more and more.

Electric cars don't need gasoline, so they don't release greenhouse gases. Another alternative is biodiesel. Biodiesel can be used in diesel engines. It is made from plants, not fossil fuels.

In the future, scientists hope to start trapping greenhouse gases and using them for fuel. This would mean burning the fuel would not release more greenhouse gases. Right now, this process is too expensive. Gasoline is much cheaper, but that might change one day.

For now, gasoline and diesel are here to stay. They power the vehicles all around us. Making them links people and companies around the world.

DID YOU KNOW?

Americans make up 4 percent of the world's population, but Americans use 35 percent of the world's gasoline.

Glossary

additives Materials that are added to something else.

by-products Things that are made during a process that are not the desired final product.

carbon dioxide A greenhouse gas that is in the air.

extract To take something out of something else.

fossil fuel A fuel that is formed in the earth from dead plants or animals.

fracking A method of extracting crude oil or natural gas from the ground by pushing water through rock.

goods Things people want to buy.

greenhouse gas A gas that causes Earth to heat up by trapping heat around it.

refined Made pure.

Find Out More

Books

Doeden, Matt. *Finding Out About Coal, Oil, and Natural Gas*. Minneapolis, MN: Lerner Classroom, 2014.

Watts, Pam. *Gasoline Engines*. How It Works. Mendota Heights, MN: Focus Readers, 2017.

Websites

What Is the Big Deal with Carbon?

https://climatekids.nasa.gov/carbon

NASA explains the importance of carbon.

What Is Gasoline Made Of?

https://wonderopolis.org/wonder/what-is-gasoline-made-of

This website gives facts about making gasoline.

Index

Page numbers in **boldface** refer to images. Entries in **boldface** are glossary terms.

About the Author

Derek Miller is an educator from Salisbury, Maryland. He loves learning how objects we use every day are engineered and sharing that knowledge with students. His other books include *How Are Smartphones Made and Sold?*